I0756238

FINISHING LINE PRESS
www.finishinglinepress.com

Marriage: A History

poems by

Bruce Parker

Finishing Line Press
Georgetown, Kentucky

Marriage: A History

poems

ISBN 979-8-89990-476-9 First Edition

ACKNOWLEDGMENTS

Grateful thanks to the editors and staffs of the following publications in which the cited poems first appeared:

Aries: A Journal of Creative Expression, "Some Rain in a Garden"
Floyd County Moonshine, "My Artist Friend Feeds the Birds"
Months to Years "Nyingma Bodhisattva Dementia"
Proud to Be: Writing by American Warriors [anthology] "Homecoming from Korea"
Scarlet Leaf Review, "Me and My Big Olds"
Tears for Things [chapbook], "Kitchen," "Solitaire"
The Field Guide Poetry Magazine, "Field Guide"
The RavensPerch, "Kintsugi, Golden Joinery"

Publisher: Leah Huete de Maines
Editor: Christen Kincaid
Cover Art: Wilderness Edge Resort, Montana, Rainbow at Sunset
by Bruce Parker
Author Photo: Lucy Cotter, PhD
Cover Design: Elizabeth Maines McCleavy

Order online: www.finishinglinepress.com
also available on amazon.com

Author inquiries and mail orders:
Finishing Line Press
PO Box 1626
Georgetown, Kentucky 40324
USA

Contents

in memoriam
Judy Tresino Parker 1945-1970
J. Louise Wheeler 1945-2014

J

The Critical List

In the ward,
the very old lie.
They breathe
and do not live,
sexless old women,
mouths agape under sightless eyes—
they breathe
and do not die.

My love, too, lies there,
scarcely moving, stirring slightly,
sleeps or stares;
her eyes reveal no thought,
numbed by pain and fever.

Tubes run to her veins,
her hair still grows.
She is lost, adrift,
her speech comes slowly, as from far away,
and if she knows she cannot say
what grim thing grips her mind and body.

I come to her each day
and gently wipe her face.
The old women do not see us.
I live my life while she lies there,
I see the void within her,
her lungs filled with thick fluid.
I feel how both choke her.
Her face is moist and hot.

Dismissing me
and turning back to work
her Black woman doctor said of her pain,
"She's been anointed."
And yet she still draws breath.

Me and My Big Olds

I had to bring a very sick wife home, after
Christmas, 1969.
He was dressed in jeans, denim jacket,
blue ball cap
she was unable to remember her address
at two A.M.
she smoked cigarettes down to her fingertips unaware
he wandered at night, dressed for church on a Tuesday
in my '59 Oldsmobile the size of an aircraft carrier
ferry her back from Parkersburg, West Virginia.
His kin didn't mind him
her folks came once to see her in hospital
I was blinded by oncoming headlights
she died unattended he was
dead before he hit the ground.
Snow covered the shoulders her kidneys were failing
two attorneys stopped and noted the time
that's the last thing you expect
at two A.M. nine P.M. the caller from the hospital said
cop said as he measured the
pneumonia, mucus plug
skid marks.

After a Funeral

She should have worn no dress she wore in life
because the things of living are for the living,
and this is something new.
She had the ring I gave her,
a futile denial of death do us part.

This calm tone betrays
the steady wailing in my heart,
as still as this white paper,
as wild as a sparrow's curse,
deep and far away as she is buried.

Solitaire

There are times one needs to read nothing at all...play solitaire.
—Diane Seuss

That was it, the time I needed to read nothing required
by English literature courses I did not attend,
played solitaire all day every day, wore out a deck of cards,
flunked because I never withdrew, the shock and numbness
of a long future abruptly interred.
I would not kiss her corpse nor agree
she looked so natural as if lying there not breathing
was an everyday thing. I needed solitaire in dumb silence
all day every day until the deck could scarcely be read.

P

Aquarium

A summer evening, thunder, the crawfish tries
to climb the glass sides of the tank in vain;
enclosed, slipping, he can utter no cries,
sees no lightning, does not know rain.
We climb the slick walls of each other's minds
uttering no cries the other can hear,
our logic hard as glass, untouched by winds,
our nameless flickering thunderous fears.
Each of us a self-enclosed storm
raging in a medium unable to
sustain the other's life, enclose its form,
twined as the crawfish and thunder, we two.
Yet should he escape the crawfish will die,
and we if we parted lose more than our lives.

Homecoming from Korea

When not working
I went on long bike rides past rice fields and woods,
so peaceful
I could hear a cuckoo call a mile off,
so quiet
the separation from you hurt a little less.
What happened to us was distance, and time,
the peace a dust that settled over everything
and *welcome home, wipe your feet, put your bag there*
dinner will be ready soon fading away
into the time and distance,
as far away as rice fields *where were you*
when I needed you

Memories Are Made of This

He knew, as he watched her come up the walk to the house,
that she had fled like the hart
after wounding him. Her face was set, not blank exactly,
her green loden coat wrapped unbuttoned around her still-
warm torso. He closed the blinds of the second-floor bedroom.
Where could he go, he wondered,
when the welcome mat was dumped in the trash?

She didn't say anything lately, just wept in a corner
while songs of her unbridled youth spun on the stereo.
He played some records, too,
you're no good, you're no good Ronstadt sang
as he mopped the kitchen floor.
Her oratorio society rehearsed Thursday evenings:
he hated Haydn *meeting in smoky places,*
hiding in shadowy corners hallelujah chorus
and he leaned on his mop handle *god I hate this place*
around the toothpick in the corner of his mouth
even though it was his own place
The Enchanted Sandwich Shop

some enchanted evening you will meet a stranger
the place was empty except for the blonde
eerily her duplicate but blonde and he
got himself a plate of food and walked over
and said *it's so crowded in here, mind if I join you* so
she smiled as he sat and looked at his food while
she told him about tomorrow's canoe trip with her boyfriend
this isn't it he thought
and went back to his mop

remembered her doppelganger come up the walk
wrapped in her mossy green coat

L

A View out the Window

A tree spreads green lace upon the gray table of the sky
in circles and swirls of branches and young leaves.
We are past the dangers of early April
when those close to us have died,
and so we may have another year.
The young leaves will flesh out
into deeper green, the gray yield to blue,
another season of fair weather, the fragillest bulwark
against the death of Spring when its blossoms
remain unseen, blindfolded by grief, birdsong muffled.

There is talk of another year or two, while
we circle round the sun in wary weavings
that secure us a weak daylight disabled
of any power to grant growth, pried
away from one another by anxiety and fear.
The young leaves will flesh out
while yet we linger, long loving, true,
our words to one another the hallmark
of a life of balance between this gossamer
web of leaves on sky and wind that leaves it ruffled.

Some Rain in a Garden

At ease we listen to drops strike leaves
and leave our thoughts of death for another day;
we hear the water creep past clods of clay
and be taken up by roots—not yet
bereaved we hear it, our ears sensitized, we say
the clouded sky weeps with joy to get
another garden filled with water and good things,
and we are able then to put off dying long enough
to live our little time and bear our little pain,
to sing a little song, to praise a little rain.

Nyingma Bodhisattva Dementia

When you got under the table and sang
you brought us to where words could not reach,
bodhisattva still
not too frail to call others into that place
you were about to enter, sweet
voice

your clear call silenced us
in the region of our minds not subject to
words

we yearned to go with you
not left behind

My Artist Friend Feeds the Birds

Scaled quail and house finches come to feed,
then mourning doves. Grief crumples the heart unexpectedly
and people begin to say you know, old fellow, you are starting
to lose it and I say I know and what worries me is
when I shed tears uselessly,
I hope I remember you then,
above all I don't want to forget you.

The quail move through the grass, up
to the bare ground where the artist scattered seed for them.
One perches on a rock and oh I don't want to forget
you and years of love.
You know, old girl, you lost your way but
you didn't lose me. Next come the mourning doves
and after a while the little peach-breasted jobs and
grief over the sunny dry brown grass which hides the quail.

Suddenly I am cold and sparrows arrive in gusts
while my friend paints a field in his studio, his hand steadied by a stick.
I pull on a sweater the color of the sky with high
white clouds spread upon it as if my friend's brush had slipped.
There is nothing to rest the eye in the dry brown grass that
reaches away to a line of trees, and I close the blind,
blind to the pull of love.

Kitchen

Sudden tears in the kitchen
putting cups on the shelf,
praise them, they have come out of hiding
as answer to a riddle.
Praise what cannot be named.

D

Interrupt Us

It might have been
we took no interest
in each other's lives,

might well have been
no touch, no warmth, no commingled joy;
no telling what might have happened

had our separate ways
gone unintersected
to other destinations

unrecorded now that
love has interfered
with all that might have been.

Kintsugi, Golden Joinery

Her face is not perfect, scored by sorrows,
eyes shattered and wet.

A cracked mirror
shows her face.

What potter
has the skill

to fit her shards together,
to seal her with golden resin?

Along comes a man who slowly learns from her,
like the archaeologist who digs in ruins, seeks fragments,
one for whom only the broken is perfect.

Emblem

A thing can be an emblem,
such as these wedding invitations on the dining table
tessellated with late afternoon sunlight,
emblazoned with the motto "We would love to have your presence"
followed by the figure of a lotus,
itself a symbol for unkillable love
so nourishing to monkeys that seize lotuses
from temple tourists we would love to have present
having received this emblem of our affection
for the way love, long dormant, can spring forth
ink on vellum, bride's words "at our wedding"
for the dear tourist to hold, an emblem made of sunlight,
to have, a thing that identifies the senders as ones
whose love is timeless as a lotus, greedy as a monkey.

The Fish Beneath the Pier

Sometimes mine is the passion of the tiny silver fish
that dart among themselves beneath the pier.
They appear as living dots, they twist and turn
but do not churn the water or leap out clear
with sides that flash, gaping mouths,
muscular flesh. My passion, too, can flicker
beneath the surface in unseen pulses of life.
Look how I swim and dart beneath your skin,
like little fish that live in the water of your life,
a school of small silver passions teeming, teeming.

Noon

In the yard, when your work subsides,
when your back is not
bent over the flower beds, or astride
soft spray on deep greenery, this hot

summer day on the move overhead,
I hear the dashing wings of a yellow butterfly as it plies
the late blooms Spring has spread
and I see on the lawn, overgrown, a red

ball some child left behind, silent, round,
a splash like a wound
that waits to be thrown, for the sound
of your return here at noon.

I wait like the plants you plunged into this soil,
I grow in sunlight, like them
remember the dark shade of your voice,
the shower of your hair about your face

as you look upon them, your race
of leaf, petal, strong stems
that hold the air in place. Until then
I grow in this small space of earth

and mingle me with
minerals and oxygen, another soft
insect in random flight,
jigging, aloft, a summer day as it falls into night.

New Intimates

There are many ways in which we speak
of love mended before a shattered bowl breaks

and ways to live in a shared room
that matter so we may not assume

contents mattered little in the broken bowl
but only that we heal

bind each other's wounds with bark and leaves
to carry on patched lives.

Speak then of how promises to love
break on the threshold of reality

room to grow and dodge thrown chairs
assume a lover's words are meant to stay

bowl over fears that misdirect the brain
heal words too new to ward off pain

leave hands along the groove of spine
live as seeds in us of mystery amiss.

Field Guide

You are my field guide to love,
its habitat and range shown by
a blue patch on the outline of North America.
You list love's call, six notes on a stave,
and note the difference in love's plumage,
male and female. You tell me of love's migration,
how it navigates by starlight and the pull
of earth's magnetic poles, how it finds
its feeding grounds, how it flies in a V,
the lakes and rivers it rests upon,
how a hunter can kill it.

Becoming

You walk across the bedroom
nude from the shower
to get clothing from your dresser
and get dressed

in motion,
a motion of delicate balance

between your coming into the world and
becoming ash and air

in a flow cherished by many, seen by few.

It is a moment in which your heart beats,
in which the trace of your body through
time and space

lingers
even as you pull on tights and shirt
and turn to walk back into
daylight as it fills the room.

The Touching Poem

Because in the long sleep to come
there will be no dreams
I touch you now
and remember touching you
and touch you now.
When I sleep
I dream of touching you;
awake, remember the dream,
the touch essential to be awake
as the Buddha said.
Now awake I dream of touching you,
remember the touch
and touch
and touch again.
You must know what you touch,
in touching know
as men and women know each other
through this touching.
I touch your feet, the tenderest place,
so when you walk and your feet touch the ground
you will know the earth and me.

Born in Providence, Rhode Island, **Bruce Parker** has published two chapbooks, *Ramadan in Summer*, (Finishing Line Press, 2022) and *Tears for Things* (Plan B Press, 2024). He holds a BA in History from the University of Maryland, Far East Division, Okinawa, Japan; and an MA in Secondary Education from the University of New Mexico. His work appears in *Triggerfish Critical Review, Wild Roof, Cerasus* (UK), *Brussels Review* (Belgium), *Prairie Schooner* and elsewhere. Married to fellow poet and artist Diane Corson, he lives in Portland, Oregon.

www.ingramcontent.com/pod-product-compliance
Lightning Source LLC
LaVergne TN
LVHW090539110826
845146LV00003B/1186

* 9 7 9 8 8 9 9 9 0 4 7 6 9 *